G000022533

THE TRUTH ABOUT YUGOSLAVIA

The Truth about
Yugoslavia

Why working people should oppose intervention

PATHFINDER

New York London Montreal Sydney

Edited by George Fyson

Copyright © 1993 by Pathfinder Press

ISBN 0-87348-776-1 paper; ISBN 0-87348-777-X cloth
Library of Congress Catalog Card Number 93-84841
Manufactured in the United States of America

First edition, 1993

Cover design by Toni Gorton
Cover photograph: Students in Belgrade demonstrate in June 1992, demanding
the resignation of President Slobodan Milosevic. (AP/Wide World Photos)

Pathfinder

410 West Street, New York, NY 10014, U.S.A.
Fax: (212) 727-0150

PATHFINDER DISTRIBUTORS AROUND THE WORLD:
Australia (and Asia and the Pacific):
    Pathfinder, 19 Terry St., Surry Hills, Sydney, N.S.W. 2010
Britain (and Europe, Africa except South Africa, and Middle East):
    Pathfinder, 47 The Cut, London, SE1 8LL
Canada:
    Pathfinder, 6566, boul. St-Laurent, Montreal, Quebec, H2S 3C6
Iceland:
    Pathfinder, Klapparstíg 26, 2d floor, 101 Reykjavík
    Postal address: P. Box 233, 121 Reykjavík
New Zealand:
    Pathfinder, La Gonda Arcade, 203 Karangahape Road, Auckland
    Postal address: P.O. Box 8730, Auckland
Sweden:
    Pathfinder, Vikingagatan 10, S-113 42, Stockholm
United States (and Caribbean, Latin America, and South Africa):
    Pathfinder, 410 West Street, New York, NY 10014

Contents

PATHFINDER MAPS BY JAY RESSLER

THE BALKANS

COUNTRY	POPULATION (millions)	GNP (billions)	PER CAPITA GNP
ALBANIA	3.3	$ 3.8	$1,200
BULGARIA	9.0	51.2	5,710
GREECE	10.1	56.3	5,605
ROMANIA	23.4	79.8	3,445
YUGOSLAVIA (1989)	23.9	129.5	5,464

Source: 1992 World Almanac

YUGOSLAVIA

	POPULATION (millions)	COMPOSITION	PERCENT OF TOTAL POPULATION	PERCENT OF TOTAL GNP
YUGOSLAVIA	22.4	36% Serb; 20% Croat; 9% Muslim; 8% Slovene; 8% Albanian; 6% Macedonian; 5% Yugoslavian (declared no other nationality); 3% Montenegrin; 2% Hungarian; 1% Gypsy	100	100
BOSNIA-HERZEGOVINA	4.1	40% Muslim; 32% Serb; 17% Croat	18.7	13.3
CROATIA	4.6	75% Croat; 12% Serb	20.1	24.6
MACEDONIA	1.9	67% Macedonian; 19% Albanian; 5% Turk	8.7	5.7
MONTENEGRO	0.6	69% Montenegrin; 14% Muslim; 6% Albanian	2.7	2.0
SERBIA (includes Kosovo and Vojvodina)	9.3	66% Serb	41.5	36.4
KOSOVO	1.6	78% Albanian; 13% Serb	—	—
VOJVODINA	2.0	54% Serb; 19% Hungarian	—	—
SLOVENIA	1.9	91% Slovene	8.3	18.0

Source: Statesman's Year-Book (1981 census, last to include figures for all regions)

Introduction

As this book goes to press, Washington is preparing to go to war in the former Yugoslavia. Its declared plans include air attacks on bridges, roads, and military positions of the rightist forces in Bosnia linked to the Serbian regime in Belgrade.

Washington has also declared its intention to send tens of thousands of troops, equipped with tanks and other armor and backed up with massive air power, to enforce a cease-fire in Bosnia.

Prior to this decision by the U.S. rulers, the British and French governments sent troops to head a military operation conducted under United Nations cover in Yugoslavia. The German government took steps to enable some of its naval and air forces to be deployed in the region—the first time since World War II it has made such moves.

These events culminate months of debating and maneuvering between the rulers in Washington, London, Paris, and Bonn over how to intervene in the former Yugoslavia. While publicly claiming humanitarian concern, each of the imperialist powers is in reality seeking to advance its own economic, political, and strategic military interests, which conflict in an increasingly sharp way during a period of world capitalist depression.

Now that Washington has decided the time is ripe to assert its might, the rivalry continues over who should command the operation. Washington wants the formal command to be under NATO, the military alliance dominated by the U.S. government and its officer corps. This course has met sharp opposition from the government of France, which is not part of NATO's military structure.

Working people and youth in the United States and around the world are asking what lies behind this war. The authors of this book present the social and economic roots of the conflict, explaining that the military plans of the rival imperialist powers hold no benefits for working people in the region or anywhere else.

*   *   *

"Tell the world this is not an ethnic war." This was the emphatic message of Ramiz Beshlija, a shepherd whose family lives on the outskirts of Sarajevo and whose neighbors are among the many of Serbian origin participating in defense of the city. Beshlija was speaking to Argiris Malapanis, a reporter for the *Militant* newsweekly who visited Sarajevo in July 1992.

Despite the murderous attacks and chauvinist campaigns conducted by rightist forces over the past two years, millions of working people in the former Yugoslavia remain deeply hostile to the notion that they must no longer live with, work alongside, and intermarry with those of different national origins, as they have done for decades.

"This is not a war between Serbs and Muslims," Haris Halilovic, a hotel worker, told Malapanis. "You can see it here," he said, pointing to families of Serbian and Croatian origin, and of the Muslim and Christian faith, crammed into a basement shelter together.

Rightist leader Radovan Karadzic, who has led the "ethnic

cleansing" in Bosnia by the Belgrade-backed forces, claims that Serbs and Muslims are instinctively hostile to each other, "like cats and dogs."

"Remarks like that are simply stupid," responded Zdravko Jovanovic, a small businessman in Sasici, a village outside the Muslim-majority town of Gorazde in eastern Bosnia. Jovanovic, who is Serbian by birth, added, "Serbs and Muslims have lived in the same valleys, used the same roads, worked in the same places, and intermarried throughout our history. Now Karadzic wants to tear us apart. You just tell him from me, come to Sasici. We'll sort him out."

In Serbia itself, the regime has had difficulty drafting youth to fight, and has faced antiwar demonstrations, including a march of 100,000 in Belgrade in June 1992 calling for negotiations to end the Belgrade-backed wars in Croatia and Bosnia.

Supporters of imperialist intervention into the Balkans perpetuate the myth of "irreconcilable national hatreds" to rationalize such involvement.

But the explanation for the conflicts in the former Yugoslavia lies not in "age-old animosities" between working people of Serbian, Croatian, or Albanian origin, or those who belong to the Muslim faith and various Christian denominations. Rather, what is happening there is a product of the crisis and growing world disorder of capitalism.

The Yugoslav workers' state that came out of the revolutionary struggle for national sovereignty and socialism in the 1940s was increasingly dominated by a privileged petty-bourgeois caste. This social layer monopolized power in the state institutions, the officer corps, and the management of the state-owned factories and other economic units. The caste encompassed individuals of every national origin in Yugoslavia and organized its control through the League of Yugoslav Communists, the ruling Stalinist party.

In 1989-91, Stalinist regimes and ruling parties crumbled across Eastern Europe and the Soviet Union, often in the face of massive popular protests. These regimes had been weakened by years of growing economic and political crisis. The Stalinist bureaucratic and anti-working-class methods of planning and management proved incapable of raising labor productivity. The resulting crisis was worsened by the deepening economic stagnation of world capitalism since the mid 1970s.

The League of Yugoslav Communists began to split up in January 1990, following a period marked by skyrocketing inflation, intractable large-scale unemployment, and mounting strike struggles. The entire bureaucratic apparatus of the party, government, and state enterprises fragmented, largely along the lines of the major provincial administrations within the former Yugoslav Federal Republic.

All the contending gangs within the privileged caste have charted a course towards integrating their economies into the world capitalist system, an increasingly difficult task in today's depression conditions. This endeavor has gone hand in hand with their attempts to begin expanding capitalist market relations in the territory they control. In this process they seek to use the leverage of their privileged political and social positions to establish themselves as the new property-owning class.

These mafia-like gangs have reached out to the various imperialist powers for loans, investments, and other assistance. In turn Bonn, Paris, London, and Washington have sought to reassert or extend their economic and political influence there and throughout the Balkan region.

In order to rally political support, Yugoslavia's aspiring capitalists have draped themselves in different nationalist flags, as they fight among themselves to maximize the territory and resources under their control.

The most aggressive force in these wars is the regime headed by Slobodan Milosevic in Serbia, whose top officials, headquartered in Belgrade, also predominated in the old Yugoslav federal state. At first they tried to use the Yugoslav army to block their rivals in the different republics from breaking away. When this failed in Slovenia in 1991, Belgrade proceeded to organize and supply armed bands to act on its behalf in those parts of Croatia and Bosnia where populations of Serbian origin predominate, with the goal of absorbing these areas and their wealth into a "Greater Serbia."

The current conflicts—fueled by rivalries among the aspiring capitalist layers at the expense of the majority of workers and farmers—had long been simmering within the previous federal regime. From early on under the presidency of Josip Broz Tito, Yugoslavia's Stalinist authorities made use of capitalist market forces in an effort to wring greater productivity from workers in the nationalized economy. Such policies encouraged competition rather than planned cooperation between the different state enterprises and republics and deepened economic and social imbalances between the different republics of Yugoslavia. Various wings of the ruling bureaucratic layer used nationalist demagogy dredged up from the late nineteenth and early twentieth centuries to claim a bigger share for themselves of the wealth produced by workers of all national origins in Yugoslavia.

But when these forces openly embarked on a course toward reestablishing capitalism, their conflicts took on a new and sharper dynamic as the leading officials in Belgrade, in the Croatian capital Zagreb, and elsewhere intensified the piracy, plunder, and killing.

The most prolonged and bloody of the battles has been in Bosnia where, under relentless bombardment, working people have been driven from the towns and villages they had occupied for generations. While working people who are Muslim make up the great majority of the victims in Bosnia, non-Muslim workers and farmers of Croatian and Serbian origin have also been targets of this "ethnic cleansing," carried out by forces either commanded directly or sponsored by Belgrade and Zagreb, as well as by the government of Bosnia itself.

By the end of 1992 the murderous assaults had created some 3 million refugees, 1.7 million of these from Bosnia. The great majority of the refugees remain within the borders of the former Yugoslavia, as governments in Europe and North America have resisted taking in more than a handful of those driven from their homes by the unending assaults.

Six months of fighting in Croatia in 1991 ended with 10,000 dead. Rightist forces, heavily armed by the Yugoslav army, had seized a third of the territory of the former republic of Croatia, proclaiming it the "Serb republic of Krajina." In January 1993 the regime in Zagreb launched a counteroffensive into a section of this area, on the Dalmatian coast. As this preface is being completed, forces commanded by Zagreb are also waging a bloody drive for increased territory in central Bosnia.

Another region where the regime in Belgrade is determined to maintain its hold regardless of the wishes of the local population is Kosovo, a southern province of Serbia that was granted autonomous status in 1974. Belgrade revoked Kosovo's autonomy in 1989 in retaliation against widespread protests by the majority-Albanian population there demanding an end to repression. Rightist groups encouraged by the Serbian government have called for "open war" on Albanians and expulsion of those who defy rule by the Belgrade regime in the region.

Both Belgrade and the Greek government have openly threatened to carve up the former Yugoslav republic of Macedonia. The capitalist rulers in Athens have made an issue of the republic's use of the name "Macedonia," demagogically charging that this signifies aggressive designs by the Macedonian government on the northern province of Greece, also known as Macedonia. Officials from Belgrade have floated a trial balloon about partitioning Macedonia, with a "leak" to the press that they had discussed this with the Greek government.

This book's authors look into these conflicts, explaining that the would-be capitalists that have emerged from the privileged caste in the former Yugoslavia are responsible for the slaughter taking place today—a slaughter imposed upon working people whose parents and grandparents made a socialist revolution in that country. The Yugoslav revolution, forged in the midst of World War II, was a social upheaval by millions. It brought an end to a period in which capitalist regimes carried out massacres against various ethnic groups. The fascist Ustashi regime set up in Croatia under the German military occupation was the chief organizer of this butchery, in which large numbers of Jews, Serbs, and Muslims were killed. The Serb monarchist forces, known as Chetniks, carried out massacres of Croats.

Workers and peasants of every nationality united to make the revolution, and in the following years succeeded in narrowing some of the extreme regional disparities in industrial development, agricultural productivity, and living standards that existed in the country. Their struggle to defeat the fascist forces, win land reform, and expropriate capitalist industry had a powerful momentum. But over time, the Stalinist misleaders eroded these gains at an accelerating pace, exacerbating social inequalities and regional disparities.

None of the actions of the warring factions anywhere in the former Yugoslavia are in the interests of working people there. Nor will imperialist intervention bring them any relief. The statements by working people of different national origins cited at the beginning of this introduction are representative of millions of workers, farmers, and youth there who recognize that their interests do not lie in the chauvinism of the gangsters who claim to be their "leaders," or in the efforts to slice up the lands where they live into ever-smaller "ethnic" partitions. And despite the "humanitarian" motives professed by Washington and other intervening imperialist powers, these capitalist regimes will bring nothing to working people in Bosnia and the other former Yugoslav republics except more deaths, destruction, denial of national sovereignty, and brutal economic exploitation.

The Russian revolution of October 1917 showed how working people of city and countryside, under the leadership of the Bolshevik Party of V.I. Lenin, could forge a new state that reached beyond the national divisions and oppression reinforced by landlords and by capitalism. Its example played a powerful role in inspiring the generations that made the Yugoslav revolution of the 1940s. That example remained despite Joseph Stalin's counterrevolutionary policies and murderous repression that drove working people out of politics from the late 1920s.

Today working people in the former Yugoslavia can look to South Africa where, under the leadership of the African National Congress, masses of ordinary working people are seeking to place their stamp on that society's future by fighting for a united and democratic South Africa, free of the narrow "ethnic" and racial divisions the rulers have imposed for so long.

The Cuban revolution provides an outstanding example of what working people, organized in defense of their interests as a class and in alliance with fellow working people internationally, can achieve. They expropriated the landlords and capitalists who exploited them and, despite military attack and economic embargo by Washington, set out to build socialism, transforming themselves and society at the same time.

It is along such lines of class struggle and internationalism that working people in Yugoslavia can defend their common class interests and reconquer what previous generations began to achieve with the revolution of the 1940s. In the process they can create a society based on human solidarity, in contrast to the rivalry, brutality, and bloody conflict that is the true product of the crisis of the world capitalist market system.

*   *   *

The contents of this book first appeared in the socialist newsweekly the *Militant* between April and October 1992. The article "Will military intervention stop the slaughter?" was written in reply to an item in the August 12, 1992, *Guardian*, a New York–based weekly that ceased publication with that issue. Much of the material, including photographs, resulted from a trip to Yugoslavia by a team of *Militant* reporters in July 1992. They visited Belgrade, Kosovo, Zagreb, Split, Dubrovnik, Sarajevo, and Skopje, as well as several cities in Greece, speaking with workers, antiwar activists, and students.

*   *   *

A note on the authors. George Fyson is editor of the *Militant* and a long-time socialist journalist from New Zealand. Argiris Malapanis, managing editor of the *Militant,* led the paper's reporting team to Yugoslavia in July 1992. Jonathan Silberman is a member of the Amalgamated Engineering and Electrical Workers Union in Manchester, England. He is a contributing editor of the magazine *New International.*

George Fyson
May 10, 1993

Chronology

1918   The Kingdom of the Serbs, Croats, and Slovenes is formed incorporating Serbia, Croatia, Dalmatia, Bosnia, Herzegovina, Slovenia, Vojvodina, and Montenegro.

1929   The country's name is changed to Yugoslavia.

1941   German troops invade and occupy Yugoslavia. Berlin sets up a puppet regime in Croatia.

November 1942   The Partisan resistance force is established, led by the Communist Party.

November 1943   The Partisans proclaim a provisional government.

October 1944   German occupation forces are driven from Yugoslavia; Partisans now number 800,000.

November 1944   A Partisan decree orders the confiscation of the property of the occupiers and their collaborators, amounting to 80 percent of industry, most banks, and almost all commercial enterprises.

1945   A joint government of Josip Broz Tito and royalist forces is established in March. Tito becomes prime minister and the monarchy is abolished. Under the impact of revolutionary mobilizations, a land reform is enacted and a workers' and peasants' government comes into being.

1945-48   Tension increases between Belgrade and Moscow as the

Tito regime refuses to subordinate Yugoslavia's economic development to that of the Soviet Union.

1948   Moscow imposes an economic blockade on Yugoslavia.

1950   Tito regime supports U.S.-led war in Korea.

1950s   A privileged bureaucratic caste consolidates its power in Yugoslavia and reaches an accommodation with Moscow.

1968   Students demonstrate for democratic rights and to oppose U.S. war in Vietnam.

1980   Tito dies and a rotating federal presidency between the republics is put into effect.

1988   Protest of 500,000 in Kosovo against abuses by the federal government in Belgrade.

Widespread strikes over declining living standards.

1989   Belgrade takes control of the courts and police in Kosovo. Hundreds of thousands in the province demonstrate in protest.

January 23 1990   Congress of Yugoslavia's ruling League of Communists (Communist Party) adjourns indefinitely. The party later breaks apart entirely.

July 1990   Belgrade dissolves the Kosovo government and takes direct control.

August 1990   A rally of 200,000 in Foca, Bosnia, protests attacks by Belgrade-backed forces.

September 1990   Protest strike of more than 100,000 in Kosovo. Belgrade formally annexes the province.

March 1991   Paramilitary police attack residents of Serbian origin in Pakrac, Croatia.

Antigovernment protests in Belgrade crest in demonstration of 100,000.

June 1991   Slovenia and Croatia formally declare independence.

Battles erupt between forces in the province of Slovenia and the federal Yugoslav army.

October 1991   Croatia and Slovenia secede from Yugoslavia.

February 1992   UN Security Council approves deployment of 14,000 troops in Croatia.

March 1992   Bosnia-Herzegovina secedes from Yugoslavia. Fighting in the war extends to Bosnia.

UN troops begin to arrive in Croatia. Operation is initially headquartered in Sarajevo.

April 5 1992   Tens of thousands demonstrate outside the multiethnic Bosnian parliament in Sarajevo, demanding an end to chauvinist violence. As news arrives of the European Community's decision to recognize Bosnia's independence, snipers of the Serbian Democratic Party kill several people and flee. That night heavy guns begin shelling the city; siege begins.

May 1992   UN estimates that the war has displaced 1.2 million people in Bosnia-Herzegovina.

Representatives of forces backed by the Belgrade and Zagreb regimes meet secretly in Austria to discuss partition of Bosnia, announce agreement to stop fighting each other to consolidate land grab.

May 29-30 1992   The Bosnian capital, Sarajevo, comes under intense bombardment by Belgrade-backed forces.

May 30 1992   UN Security Council votes to impose sanctions on Serbia.

May 31 1992   Belgrade regime holds parliamentary elections; 50,000 march in Belgrade to demand ouster of President Slobodan Milosevic.

June 28 1992   March of 100,000 in Belgrade demands an end to the war in Bosnia.

July 1992   NATO powers agree to tighten the trade embargo imposed on Serbia by the UN.

March 1993   NATO members meet to discuss a U.S. proposal to ready 50,000 troops for deployment in Bosnia. UN troop deployments had reached 16,000 by early 1993.

May 1 1993   The White House announces plans to use U.S. fighter-bombers against Serbian forces in Bosnia.

ROOTS OF THE CONFLICT

The roots of the conflict in Yugoslavia

by George Fyson and Jonathan Silberman

Yugoslavia is gripped by a murderous conflict orchestrated above all by the regime in Serbia, as well as by leaders of Croatia and other republics. Yugoslav working people, who almost five decades ago began a mighty socialist revolution, are the ones who are paying with their lives.

Into this situation the rival imperialist powers of Europe and the United States are seeking ways to intervene, wield their forces, and place their stamp on the outcome of events. Acting through the United Nations, they placed an embargo on Serbia in May 1992 and at the beginning of 1993 were weighing the prospects of military involvement substantially beyond the UN forces already stationed there.

The military conflict in Yugoslavia began in June 1991, when skirmishes in Slovenia were followed by a devastating war in Croatia, where some 10,000 people were killed. In March 1992 the slaughter began in Bosnia-Herzegovina. Indiscriminate massacres of civilians and devastation of cities to a degree not seen since Washington's war against Iraq resulted in at least 7,000 deaths in the first three months of the year. (In mid-1992, the government of Bosnia-Herzegovina put the death toll as high as 50,000.)

The war had created as many as 1 million refugees in Croatia, and some 1.2 million in Bosnia-Herzegovina by mid-1992. The number of refugees in Bosnia-Herzegovina—estimated at one quarter of its population—is the highest anywhere in Europe since World War II. The former Yugoslavia had a population of 24 million.

Capitalist-minded political commentators argue that the current conflicts in Yugoslavia are the modern expression of centuries of tribal or ethnic strife that has gripped this part of the world. They use this claim to justify the need for outside intervention in the form of an economic embargo and possible military attack. The people of Yugoslavia, they say, are helpless to solve on their own the problems they face.

The truth is the opposite. Today's conflicts in Yugoslavia have nothing in common with the historic rise of nation-states that accompanied the bourgeois-democratic revolutions against feudal conditions in the period from the sixteenth to the early twentieth century. Nor are they similar to modern national liberation struggles against colonialism and imperialist oppression. Instead, what is involved is a crude drive for control over territory and resources between the conflicting bureaucratic gangs that rule in the regions of the former Yugoslavia.

As in the former Soviet Union and elsewhere in Eastern Europe, elements of the old Stalinist bureaucracy have discarded their previous verbal claims to "communism" as easily as a snake sheds its old skin. Now they are acting as would-be capitalists to grab as big a portion of the loot as they can, just as any mafia operates to protect and enlarge its turf. And they are competing among themselves for a poor cousin's place at the table of world capitalism.

The main aggressors on the Yugoslav battleground are the bureaucrats based in Serbia, the dominant republic in the former Yugoslavia, whose largest city, Belgrade, had been the federal capital.

ARGIRIS MALAPANIS/MILITANT

Ramiz Beshlija, a shepherd living on the outskirts of Sarajevo, points to destruction from bombardment. "Tell the world this is not an ethnic war," he said.

ARGIRIS MALAPANIS/MILITANT

War victims in Sarajevo. Nurse at right lost her leg when Belgrade-backed forces shelled breadline.

The regimes in Croatia and the other republics have shown themselves to be no less keen to plunder resources for themselves, as the Croatian regime's annexation of a piece of Bosnia-Herzegovina in July 1992 demonstrated.

None of the fights being waged by the regimes and their surrogate forces in Yugoslavia today are in the interests of working people there, whose parents and grandparents carried out a powerful revolution in the 1940s, a revolution that overturned the rule of the exploiting landlords and capitalists of different tongues and creeds, and forged a united Yugoslavia.

The conflicts since 1991 have been noteworthy for the inability of the regimes to mobilize large numbers of working people to fight; for the large number of desertions from the Yugoslav army; for the cases of fraternization between soldiers and those they were supposed to be fighting; and for the protests against the war, especially in Belgrade. In June 1992 alone, tens of thousands took part in protests against the war, including one rally of 100,000.

Despite the nationalist demagogy of the would-be capitalists, what is taking place is not national, religious, ethnic, or tribal struggle. It is the *modern class struggle*.

The petty-bourgeois and aspiring bourgeois layers in Belgrade and elsewhere are interested only in safeguarding their own privileges, diverting workers from acting in their own class interests, and continuing the fruitless attempt to be welcomed as equal partners into the world capitalist system.

Today this is a less realistic perspective than ever. The world capitalist system is in the initial throes of a historic crisis. Instability, economic depression, social crisis, and war are what this system holds in store.

The events in Yugoslavia are not the product of communism. The Yugoslav crisis is one in a series that has gripped the deformed and degenerated workers' states in eastern and central Europe and the former Soviet Union since the late 1980s, bringing down governments and shattering the ruling Stalinist parties.

Today the components of the former Yugoslavia have an enormous debt to imperialist banks and financial institutions, rampant inflation, and massive unemployment. Yugoslav workers have been forced to migrate in search of work. Even before the wave of war-generated refugees in 1992, there were 600,000 Yugoslav workers in Germany alone.

Different sections of the ruling stratum in Yugoslavia advance variations on a single approach to getting out of the mess the country is in. Although they drape their rhetoric in different "national" colors, they share the desire to shove the effects of the crisis onto the backs of working people.

Out of the class struggles that will inevitably result, workers will have their chance to build communist parties capable of leading revolutionary anticapitalist struggles to establish governments of the workers and farmers and join in the worldwide fight for socialism. The future battles that workers face in the former Yugoslavia, in overthrowing the parasitic caste that today presides over the bloody dismemberment of the federation, are *part* of this worldwide struggle.

The tasks working people face can be best appreciated by reviewing the road they have already traveled—what the workers and peasants achieved in the Yugoslav revolution of the latter part of the 1940s, and how that revolution was betrayed.

The rise, accomplishments, and degeneration of the Yugoslav revolution

The Yugoslav revolution is one of the historic conquests of the working class, just like the Russian revolution of 1917, the Chinese revolution of 1949, and the Cuban revolution of 1959. It was a mighty "festival of the oppressed," as Lenin described the Bolshevik-led October revolution in Russia. The revolutionary example set by the toilers in Russia and elsewhere in the old tsarist empire inspired generations of working-class leaders in Yugoslavia.

Yugoslavia was an economically backward country at the time of the revolution. Indeed the Balkans, which comprise Albania, Bulgaria, Greece, Romania, and Yugoslavia, were the most backward part of Europe. The region accounted for just 2.5 percent of European industrial production, most of this closely connected with agriculture—milling, wine-pressing, and manufacture of vegetable oils. About 80 percent of the Yugoslav population of 16 million were peasants, 1 million of whom were landless and worked as migratory, seasonal farm workers.

The land was in the hands of a few large landowners, and the peasantry was oppressed by the hangovers of semifeudal conditions onto which the harshest of capitalist social relations had been grafted. Agricultural taxes in the Balkans were among the highest in the world. The mortgage and loan debts of the peasants were enormous. Interest rates for seed and tools in the region ran up to 80 percent. In some areas the peasants were still engaged in subsistence farming. The modern working class numbered at most 100,000.

Yugoslavia was dominated by foreign capital, first British and French, and then by growing German interests in the 1920s and 1930s. It was effectively a semicolony of these European imperialist powers, with its economic and social development held back in their interests.

Yugoslavia was united as a country at the end of World War I with the coming together of six republics under the Serbian monarchy. The Kingdom of Serbs, Croats, and Slovenes, established in 1918, took the name Yugoslavia in 1929. When World

War II opened, there was little or no all-Yugoslav industrial infrastructure. Within this framework, the north and west were relatively more modern and advanced, the south more backward.

The legacy of colonial domination by the "European" Austro-Hungarian Empire or by the "Asian" Ottoman Empire—as the bourgeois press insists on designating these powers—left its mark in the form of different languages and alphabets, ethnic origins, and religions. Serbia, home of the oppressive Karageorgevich monarchy, dominated Croatia, Bosnia-Herzegovina, Kosovo, Macedonia, Montenegro, Slovenia, and Vojvodina. National oppression was enshrined in law. There was no separation between the state and the church—between the state and the hierarchy of the Serbian-based Orthodox Church of Yugoslavia, that is.

The workers' movement was weak, beset by both the objective backwardness of the country and harsh repression. Many political oppositionists were imprisoned; some were executed.

Despite the weakness of the organized Communist Party and workers' movement, the 1917 Russian revolution had great prestige there. Yugoslav peasants and youth were attracted by the revolution's agrarian reform and by its broader democratic and social conquests. In the brief democratic interlude following the country's formation after World War I, the Communist Party grew rapidly. By 1920 it had 60,000 members and in the elections of that year the party came in third, winning 12 percent of the vote. But a period of severe repression followed. By the outbreak of World War II, the Communist Party—which was underground or semilegal from 1921 onward, and whose leadership spent many years out of the country—numbered about 12,000, with 30,000 in the Communist youth organization. It had also gone through a qualitative political transformation through its adherence to the course of the Stalin-led Communist International.

This was the general condition of Yugoslavia at the outbreak of World War II. In April 1941 the Axis powers invaded—primarily German troops, assisted by Italian, Bulgarian, and Hungarian forces. The Axis occupation won the support of the Yugoslav landowners and capitalists in their majority; the rise of German imperialist domination had ensured their pro-Berlin orientation.

Prior to the Axis invasion, the Karageorgevich monarchy had concluded an agreement with Hitler. Forces within the army officer corps then ousted the government in a coup. The king fled, along with the "royal purse." The new government, which proclaimed neutrality, organized no resistance to the Axis forces that soon crossed its borders. After eleven days, including the horrific bombing of Belgrade (which ranks alongside the devastation of Coventry and Dresden), the German occupation was complete.

In the Croatian capital of Zagreb a fascist regime under nationalist colors, the Ustashi, was established. It actively collaborated with the occupation forces, carrying out mass killings of Gypsies, Jews, and Serbs.

The Serbian monarchy set up shop in Britain. Pro-monarchy forces, known as Chetniks, established a guerrilla operation under the royalist general Draza Mihailovic. They received financial and military aid from the Allied powers—the governments of Britain, the United States, and the Soviet Union.

The principal opposition to the occupying forces was the armed Partisans. Led by the Yugoslav Communist Party, the Partisan movement was a national liberation army. It was originally set up to harass the occupying forces, not to launch an insurrectionary struggle. This was in line with dictates from the Stalin regime in Moscow, which had recognized the occupation administration and was looking to avert a German invasion of the Soviet Union.

The Yugoslav party, now headed by the Croatian-born Josip Broz Tito, followed Moscow's instructions, establishing small armed units at first. It had no intention then to take power, nor any idea that within four years it would be in power.

But the armed resistance to both the homegrown and occupying fascist forces proved tremendously popular, and the peasant masses pressed for broader social goals. Following the German invasion of the Soviet Union, Stalin gave the go-ahead to the Partisans to organize a military struggle, calling on them to act jointly with Mihailovic's Chetniks and all forces opposed to the occupation.

Workers and peasants poured into the ranks of the Partisans, who waged a courageous struggle that tied down thirty-three Axis divisions—some 500,000 troops. The fight was bitter and hard: nearly two million Yugoslavs, more than a tenth of the population, died in the war.

In the course of the successful struggle, popular committees were elected to administer liberated zones, organizing education, health care, and munitions production. Peasants seized the land of landowners who had fled or collaborated with the occupying armies. As liberated zones became linked, a newspaper began to be published three times a week, a railway system was organized, and a mail system established. In November 1942 a broad national body based on elected representatives of the popular committees was established—the Anti-Fascist Council of People's Liberation, or AVNOJ (pronounced Avnoy).

A year later, in November 1943, AVNOJ proclaimed a provisional government and announced that the king could not return. At the same time, at the meeting of U.S. president Franklin Roosevelt, British prime minister Winston Churchill, and Soviet leader Joseph Stalin in Tehran, the Allied powers first agreed that influence in postwar Yugoslavia would be shared equally between the imperialist allies and Moscow.

By late 1942 the Partisans numbered 150,000. By the end of 1943 they had grown to 300,000, and by the end of the war they were effectively a full-fledged army numbering 800,000.

The Partisans took on the character of a mass social movement. Without aid from any outside source, the movement won working people from every nationality. This included substantial recruitment of prisoners of war and deserters from the German, Italian, Bulgarian, and Hungarian armies, a recruitment policy that became the subject of sharp criticism from Moscow.

The Partisans took steps to mobilize women in the struggle, organizing two national conferences for this purpose. The predominance of young fighters was reflected in the peasants' description of the armed Partisan detachments as "the youth."

The big majority of fighters were peasants, including in the Proletarian Brigades, which formed the backbone of the Partisan army. Many workers from the cities joined the brigades and other Partisan units as well. The Proletarian Brigades were the first fighting units that were not restricted to operations in a particular region.

In uniting the toilers from every nationality behind the antifascist struggle, the Partisans advanced a program that struck at the heart of national privilege and went a long way to overcoming national enmities. It called for equality and mutual respect for all nationalities and opposed chauvinism and the domination of one nation over others.

The Partisans combined this with the objective of implementing social and economic advances in the interests of working people. They also looked beyond old "Yugoslavia" and presented the perspective of a broader Balkan federation.

The success of this approach in uniting working people in the Partisan movement confirmed in life that defense of national rights and opposition to national privilege are not the path toward nationalism, but the only road to unite the working class in the *internationalist* fight for socialism.

This stance allowed the Partisans to win over masses of peasants and workers from the murderous Croatian fascists and Serbian nationalist forces. In the town of Foca in Bosnia, for example, Ustashi forces in May 1941 killed all residents of Serbian origin who had not fled. Six months later a Partisan unit, made up of toilers of Serbian and Croatian nationality, seized the city. They tried and executed Ustashi members who were guilty of these crimes but did not take action against anyone on the basis of their nationality. Then the capitalist-led Chetniks defeated the Partisans and captured the town. They, in turn, killed everyone of Croatian origin they could round up.

When the "Big Three"—London, Washington, and the Stalin regime in the Soviet Union—demanded the restoration of the monarchy at the end of the war, Tito agreed in early 1945 to a joint government responsible to a regency—a representative of the crown—whose members would be approved by the national committee of the AVNOJ. The AVNOJ would have full legislative powers until a constituent assembly convened to make final decisions. A joint government of Tito and Ivan Subasic, prime minister of the royal government-in-exile in London, was established in March 1945.

At the same time, the revolutionary mobilization by the Partisans encroached on capitalist property relations more and more. A Partisan decree of November 24, 1944, ordered the confiscation of the property of occupiers, including extensive German capital, and their Yugoslav collaborators. This amounted to 80 percent of industry, most banks, and almost all large commercial enterprises. The subsequent nationalization law of December 1946 largely registered an already existing fact.

The new government also enacted a massive land reform in August 1945. It confiscated the property of the great landowners without compensation and put 95 percent of cultivated land into the hands of working peasants.

The government instituted steps toward economic planning, including a state monopoly of foreign trade. It took measures that during the initial years of the revolution substantially narrowed the gap between different parts of the country.

This increasingly anticapitalist course made clear that Subasic and the four other representatives of the capitalists and landed nobility had no real sway in the government. It was acting as a workers' and peasants' government on the momentum of the revolutionary struggle. Power was in the hands of the Communist Party, the leading force in the AVNOJ.

The capitalist figures resigned over the course of 1945, including Subasic. In the fall of 1945, the monarchy was abolished—implementing the AVNOJ decision of two years earlier—and the capitalist parties boycotted the November 11 elections to the constituent assembly because they knew they would be heavily defeated. The new Federal People's Republic was installed on November 29 and the new constitution adopted on January 31, 1946.

In the course of implementing these anticapitalist measures, and propelled by the mobilizations of workers and peasants that went along with them, a workers' state was established in Yugoslavia—a state based on the workers' successful conquest of state property in the basic means of production, a thoroughgoing land reform, economic planning, and a state monopoly of foreign trade.

To lead this revolution through to completion, the Partisans had to break from the attempts by Moscow to choke off the struggle of the toilers in Yugoslavia. Stalin's policies subordinated the interests of the working class and its allies in Yugoslavia—and everywhere else—to the interests of the materially privileged bureaucratic caste in the Soviet Union.

For the Moscow bureaucrats, the task of Communist parties in other countries was to do whatever was necessary and expedient to advance the shifting foreign policy needs of the Soviet regime. This was justified in the guise of "defending" the Soviet Union. Under the banner of "socialism in one country," the Communist International was transformed by Stalin into a tool for the counter-revolutionary diplomacy of the Soviet government. In May 1943 Stalin dissolved the Comintern altogether to emphasize to Washington and London that Moscow had no thought whatsoever of attempting to extend the world socialist revolution.

During World War II Stalin wished above all to maintain the alliance with Washington and London. To prove his reliability, Stalin used Moscow's influence and the Communist parties in various countries to ensure that revolutionary struggles against capitalism were defeated. In relation to Yugoslavia, Stalin closely followed Churchill's and Roosevelt's dictates.

"It seems that Great Britain and the Yugoslav government [in London] have good reasons to suspect the partisan movement of having a *communist* character and aiming at a sovietization of Yugoslavia," said a Comintern letter to Tito in 1942. "Why have you created, for instance, a special *proletarian* brigade? At the present moment, the main duty is to merge all anti-nazi trends."

The Partisans were not mentioned in the Soviet press, their radio broadcasts were censored; until 1944 they were refused any aid by the Soviet Union. The CP was urged to organize jointly with the Chetniks, and Moscow publicly supported the return of the monarchy to Yugoslavia. At three international conferences— Tehran in November-December 1943, Yalta in February 1945, and Potsdam in July 1945—Stalin reaffirmed his commitment to divide influence over postwar Yugoslavia fifty-fifty between London and Moscow.

The Yugoslav CP did not enter the struggle with the intention of breaking from Moscow. Its leadership had been trained in the Soviet Union or by Stalin's secret police in the Spanish civil war. In 1937, on orders from the Kremlin, the entire Central Committee of the party with the exception of Tito was purged. Tito himself had spent two years in Moscow and had become leader of the party only following Stalin's murder of the previous leader, Milan Gorkic. The party had followed each of Stalin's previous twists and turns.

Faithful to this approach, the program of the first session of the AVNOJ in 1942 guaranteed "no radical changes whatsoever in the social life and activities of the people." But the CP leadership's determination to lead the antifascist resistance and to defend itself, backed by a sweeping revolutionary mobilization of the toilers, led it to make political shifts as events unfolded.

An alliance with the Chetniks proved impossible. As early as November 1941, the Chetniks were organizing armed actions against the Partisans, and as the war progressed the overwhelming bulk of the Chetniks' operations were of this character.

The Yugoslav CP leadership, based on its own apparatus that more and more took on the character of a government, charted a course independent from Moscow's directives, while continuing to subscribe to a Stalinist political framework.

This independent course was important in bringing the struggle in Yugoslavia to an outcome different from what happened in Greece, where the CP did carry out Stalin's orders. The Greek partisans were disarmed under the British occupation; the struggle was then drowned in blood. The Yugoslav CP was also from the Stalinist stable, but it was able to lead a determined fight for national liberation that, in the exceptional circumstances of war and foreign occupation, ensured the success of the anticapitalist revolution.

The emerging imperialist war victors were alarmed by this development. The revolution meant more than just material conquests for the Yugoslav toilers, important as these were. Its success engendered solidarity by fighting workers and youth around the world. Revolutionaries in other countries reached out to defend and assist the Yugoslav revolution.

Thousands of workers and youth went on work brigades to Yugoslavia to build roads, railroads, and other public works. In the summer of 1950, 3,000 people from France were organized in the Jean Jaurès Brigade, the Rosa Luxemburg Brigade, and the Renault Brigade made up of auto workers from the Renault Billancourt plant near Paris. Brigades went from Britain and elsewhere in Europe, and plans were made for a U.S. brigade that never came to fruition.

Imperialism reacted to the Yugoslav revolution with economic pressure, hostile propaganda, and overt military threats. Between July 16 and August 8, 1946, Yugoslav airspace was violated 172 times by British and U.S. bombers and fighters. But the postwar relationship of forces did not permit a direct imperialist military intervention.

The revolution in Yugoslavia was not the only social overturn that came out of World War II. In Albania a popular revolutionary struggle of a similar character achieved success in 1944. A worker and peasant insurgency continued to threaten capitalist rule in Greece, and was finally defeated only in 1949.

The wartime victories over fascism spurred massive mobilizations throughout Europe. In Italy the workers and peasants were armed and in a position to press for a government of the toilers. The Communist Party, however, was a major force in the coalition government that followed the fall of Mussolini and was determined to preserve its bloc with the capitalist parties. The CP organized the disarming and demobilization of working people, thus saving capitalist rule.

The victorious Soviet army's sweep through Bulgaria, Czechoslovakia, Hungary, Poland, Romania, and eastern Germany prompted a wave of workers' struggles and mass uprisings. The first response of the Kremlin was to move quickly to crush the developing independent movements and to prevent radical social transformations and the overturn of capitalist property relations. Coalition governments were set up with the most prominent capitalist politicians who would go along.

Stalin's goal was to implant pliant coalition regimes in order to use Eastern Europe as a buffer zone to protect the USSR against future invasions, while at the same time preserving capitalism in an attempt to maintain the wartime alliance with British and U.S. imperialism.

The Kremlin also imposed its own "war reparations," dismantling factories and taking them to the Soviet Union, siphoning off cash and raw materials, carrying away products to the USSR, and establishing joint economic enterprises—to Moscow's economic benefit—with the new governments that were under Soviet control. The property of the old landlord classes was expropriated and agrarian reforms were carried out, but with the objective of removing obstacles to the development of capitalism.

Stalin thought he had secured imperialist agreement with this course in the secret accord reached with the U.S. and British governments in July–August 1945 at Potsdam. Building on earlier conferences at Tehran and Yalta, the Potsdam agreement set down guidelines for maintaining the wartime alliance, dividing the spoils of war, and parceling up Europe: London and Washington would run Western Europe through traditional economic penetration; Eastern Europe would fall into the Kremlin's sphere of influence; and Germany, to be destroyed as an economic power, would be run as a joint military enterprise of the three, with a minor cut for France.

Washington and London, however, had different plans. They acted to prevent the workers' struggles that were exploding across the continent from being victorious. They encouraged the local capitalist classes in Eastern and Central Europe to use whatever political leverage they had to the detriment of Moscow. They sent troops to Greece to crush the workers' and peasants' movement.

Potsdam crashed on the rocks of reality. An "agreement" could not hold back the class struggle. The colonial revolution was advancing. The division of Europe was shutting off Eastern Europe from capitalist penetration. The criminal deindustrialization and plunder of Germany was dragging down the rest of Europe economically too. London could not play the role of world power assigned to it; its decline was sharply exposed in its inability to hold the line in Greece or in any way contribute to European economic reconstruction. Meanwhile, in the United States a labor upsurge developed.

The U.S. rulers made a sharp turn in foreign policy. The changing relationship of forces within the imperialist camp coming out of the Second World War—the military supremacy and industrial monopoly of Washington, the relative decline of London and Paris—convinced Washington to go onto the offensive.

This was codified in a bellicose March 1947 speech by President Harry Truman branding the Soviet Union an "aggressor." The wartime alliance was definitively over. (Churchill had made his "Iron Curtain" speech along the same lines at Fulton, Missouri, a year earlier).

In a series of actions that came to be called the "Truman Doctrine," Washington committed huge forces to Europe, including active intervention against the Greek insurgents. The Central Intelligence Agency was established in 1947, and the foundations were laid for the formation of the NATO military alliance between the North American and major European imperialist powers in 1949. The new militarization drive was accompanied by a renewed antilabor and red-baiting drive at home.

The "economic" complement to the Truman Doctrine was provided by the Marshall Plan, named after U.S. secretary of state George Marshall. This paved the way for the reconstruction of Europe through Germany. U.S. imperialism pushed aside Britain and France, its junior wartime allies, in an effort to unify and develop capitalist Europe under its own banner.

Stalin's response in Eastern Europe was to order the local Stalinist parties to abolish the coalition governments and carry out the expropriation of capitalist property—a popular move given the unemployment, inflation, and social dislocation following the war. Tight bureaucratic control, backed by the occupying Soviet army and the use of secret police forces based on the Kremlin model, held the active participation and mobilization of the masses in this expropriation within the limits set by Moscow. In this way there came into being several workers' states deformed at birth.

This was Europe as the 1940s drew to a close: successful popular revolutions in Yugoslavia and Albania, civil war in Greece, social overturns in Eastern Europe, unresolved conflicts between the victorious wartime imperialist powers.

In 1948 a fierce struggle that had been developing between Moscow and Belgrade broke out into the open. Moscow criticized policies of the Belgrade government and dredged up conflicts from the civil war and before; the Yugoslav leadership condemned Moscow's plunder of the so-called buffer zone of Eastern Europe.

But the split was not over political perspectives. The open breach developed because Moscow sought to impose on Belgrade the Soviet bureaucracy's "national" interests. It insisted that Yugoslavia's economic development be subordinated to the need to rebuild the Soviet Union and it opposed independent political initiatives by the Yugoslav regime. Moscow feared that if Tito's attempts to establish a Balkan federation were successful, such a group of workers' states not completely under its control could present an alternative pole to the current Kremlin clique—in the world and in the Soviet Union itself.

These conflicts brought Yugoslavia's relations with the Soviet Union to a point of extreme tension. Moscow imposed an economic blockade and conducted threatening troop movements on the border. It recruited agents inside Yugoslavia for operations against its opponents, including assassination, and attempted to organize a coup against the Yugoslav regime.

Between July 1, 1948, and September 1, 1949, there were 219 armed incidents on Yugoslavia's eastern borders. Stalin and his supporters declared Tito to have been an agent of the Nazi secret police, the Gestapo, and vilified "Titoism" internationally. For example, in a series of purge trials conducted in the late 1940s in Czechoslovakia against a section of the bureaucracy, the defendants were denounced as "Trotskyite-Titoist-Zionist bourgeois nationalist traitors."

Marxists at the time sought to counter the hysterical worldwide campaign that was launched against Tito, aimed at cutting off the support and sympathy the Yugoslav revolution had gained among revolutionary-minded workers and youth. They reached out to the Yugoslav workers and farmers, seeking to present a political course that would deepen the revolution. The Socialist Workers Party of the United States explained in an August 1948 statement:

The open break between the Cominform [the Communist Information Bureau, the Communist International's short-lived successor] and the Communist Party of Yugoslavia is the clearest expression to date of the deep crisis convulsing Stalinism.... Revolutionists can only hail this development—this first rift in the ranks of world Stalinism which must unfold in open view of the world working class.... What is more, it confronts the rank and file of the Yugoslav CP and of Stalinist parties elsewhere with the need of reexamining the ideas and the methods of Stalinism.

But the Yugoslav leadership did not turn toward the world's toilers. Instead, the Tito leadership acted to brake the forward motion of the revolution and hastened its bureaucratic degeneration. Although Tito had broken with Stalin, he had not abandoned the class-collaborationist politics of national socialism he had learned in the school of Stalinism.

The Yugoslav regime carried out a foreign policy of conciliation toward imperialism. The Yugoslav CP had never had a proletarian internationalist perspective. For five years after World War II, for example, Yugoslavia kept 100,000 German prisoners of war—workers and farmers conscripted into Hitler's armed forces—forcing them to work on road building and other economic reconstruction projects. (German prisoners of war were kept throughout Eastern and Central Europe.)

Belgrade lent credence to the U.S.-organized war to block national unification and social revolution in Korea. In 1950, the Yugoslav regime joined Washington and its allies in denouncing the workers' and peasants' government that had come to power in northern Korea for its "aggression" against the U.S.-imposed puppet government in the southern half of the country. Tito demanded that Chinese forces withdraw from Korea, while supporting the presence of the U.S. fleet off the coast of China.

While sharply at odds with Stalin, the Yugoslav leaders also joined him in stabbing the Greek revolution in the back. They closed Yugoslavia's borders and halted all aid to the Greek fighters because the Greek Communist Party supported Moscow. Tito subsequently declared Yugoslavia neutral during Washington's war against Vietnam.

In the late 1950s, after Nikita Khrushchev had become Soviet head of state following Stalin's death, an accommodation was reached between Moscow and Belgrade. These relations, however, always remained within the framework of satisfying the separate interests of the bureaucratic caste in Yugoslavia.

Foreign policy is always an extension of domestic policy, and Tito was no exception in this regard. The secret police, modeled on its Soviet counterpart, was used to silence most opposition in the party and society. While the repression did not reach the levels in the Soviet Union in the 1930s, the secret police nevertheless became a cornerstone of the corrupt and ruthless regime.

Capitalist methods of competition among enterprises and profitability were institutionalized in industry, packaged as "workers' self-management." Market mechanisms were extolled. A private market for peasant trade was widely extended. As a result, Yugoslavia began to import coal and all manner of agricultural goods that the country could itself have produced, since particular enterprises did not find it sufficiently profitable to produce these items. The state monopoly of foreign trade was allowed to erode.

Ernesto Che Guevara, a central leader of the Cuban revolution, remarked after his visit to Yugoslavia in 1959 that "the enterprises compete among themselves in the national market as if they were private capitalist entities."

Within a short period of time, social differentiation began to widen. Those who benefited were first and foremost layers of state, party, army, and management bureaucrats. Also favored were a layer of rich peasants and the professional petty-bourgeoisie, some skilled workers, property owners, and artisans from the prewar days who rapidly became the privileged technicians of the new economy.

Unemployment and part-time work, often designated as "unpaid vacations," grew. The gulf between rich and poor in Yugoslavia began to approach that of a capitalist country with a comparable level of development.

What these developments signified was that by the mid-1950s a bureaucratic caste, the Yugoslav counterpart of the ones existing in the Soviet Union and other Eastern European workers' states, had consolidated itself at the head of government and in society.

This privileged social layer enjoys incomes and access to goods and services far greater than that of ordinary working people. While it remains a minority of the population, it is nevertheless a broad social grouping. It exists as a parasitic layer, playing no special or necessary role in society other than to use its position to guarantee its own perks and privileges. The resources of the state make up the trough from which it feeds.

The privileged bureaucracy has differentiations within itself. At one end are those with the higher positions in smaller institutions in society such as productive enterprises; educational, health, and other such institutions; and the cultural establishment, including leading artists, performers, and sports stars. At the other end are the administrative chiefs of the state, ruling party, and army.

The caste is a petty-bourgeois social layer, standing between the working people on the one hand, and world imperialism on the other. Its members share bourgeois aspirations, habits, and values, often aping the lifestyles of capitalist layers in Western countries.

The Yugoslav bureaucracy—like its counterparts in Russia and elsewhere—was from early on a breeding ground for regional competition. The bureaucrats in the most advanced regions used nationalist demagogy as a weapon for self-enrichment—demanding control of the spoils of foreign investment and of trade conducted across their international borders, for example.

In the 1960s and 1970s, a section of the bureaucracy in Croatia called for income from the lucrative tourist industry of the Dalmatian coast area to be allocated entirely to the Croatian, not the federal, government. They resisted using such resources to even out the imbalances across Yugoslavia by advancing the less-developed regions.

Provinces and republics closed their markets to one another, seeking to become self-sufficient. This inevitably worked to the detriment of the least-developed regions. By 1985, for example, the income of the average resident of Slovenia was 70 percent higher than that of the average resident of Macedonia; by 1989, it was 125 percent more.

The historical roots of national divisions in Yugoslavia had been dealt huge blows by the revolution. But the bureaucrats began the process that they continue today—to do their utmost to revive the old nationalist causes, seeking to mobilize workers and farmers around their reactionary appeals, for the purpose of holding onto power and expanding the resources under their own control.

Their ability to do this has been limited by the deep-rooted gains of the Yugoslav revolution, which is seen in the extent to which, despite the appeals of the demagogues, large layers of working people do not see themselves as "Croatian," "Serbian," or some other nationality, and refuse to endorse the chauvinist course laid out by the bureaucrats. A common response is, "We are Yugoslavs, not Croats or Serbs."

In proportion as social inequality grew and tensions developed—between working people and the rising parasitic caste; between the rulers of different regions; and within the bureaucracy as a whole—the Yugoslav bureaucrats needed a powerful arbiter, standing over society as a whole, to secure their rule. In this situation Tito, a figure with great authority deriving from his identification with the revolution, was able to emerge as a Bonapartist leader. In this role he straddled the interests of the caste and the workers and peasants, keeping in check the interests of the bureaucrats, and functioning as the supreme arbiter within the caste itself.

Workers, students confront bureaucracy as economic crisis sharpens and national divisions reemerge

Protests by workers and students in Yugoslavia emerged in the 1960s, focusing especially on the new privileges of the ruling social layer. The protests began to spread on a Yugoslavia-wide basis. Forty thousand students occupied the University of Belgrade in 1968, promoting a petition that opposed the rulers' privileges and calling for democratic rights. The petition was then signed by 200,000 students around the country. The students also opposed the U.S. war in Vietnam in the face of official government neutrality.

Over the next four years a deep economic slump set in, the product of the slowdown in world capitalism and bureaucratic mismanagement.

Following the worldwide recession of 1974-75, the economic crisis intensified. Investment declined, the foreign debt escalated, production fell, and unemployment grew rapidly. By 1985 the average wage was only 40 percent of what was officially considered necessary to support a family of four at 1979 living standards. Inflation skyrocketed to an annual rate of 2,500 percent by January 1990.

From the end of 1989 to mid-1991, the Yugoslav economy contracted by more than 40 percent. A number of local governments and enterprises announced bankruptcy.

What led to the disintegration and resulted in the bloody conflicts that have raged since 1991 was not Tito's death in 1980, but the drastic economic decline. However, the Bonapartist ruler's demise did mark a turning point in the acceleration of the centrifugal forces in Yugoslavia.

These strains finally shattered the ruling Communist Party. The party was formally dissolved in early 1990. Many members left before its final breakup, declaring themselves to be Croatian nationalists, Slovenian nationalists, or some other variant. The caste in

Belgrade demagogically advanced Serbian nationalist goals, often behind the cloak of being the defender of "Yugoslavia."

This process has amounted to the bureaucracy restructuring itself—redividing and reapportioning the loot, the caste's pillage of the social surplus, among itself—and using workers and peasants as unwilling pawns in their bloody turf war.

At the same time as each wing of the bureaucracy has sought to gain control over more resources, they all cherish hopes of linking up with those they have the closest economic relations with among the imperialist powers. Depending on which wing of the caste and which region, this may be either the ruling capitalist families of Germany, France, or other countries.

The Belgrade bureaucracy's first sharp use of nationalist demagogy was in response to protests by working people and students in the Kosovo region of Serbia. People of Albanian ethnic origin make up 90 percent of the population of Kosovo, and they are victims of sharp social and economic discrimination by the Serbian authorities.

In November 1988 a march of 500,000 in Kosovo's main city, Pristina, demanded an end to second-class treatment of the province's Albanian population. The march was headed by miners carrying pictures of Tito and Yugoslav, Albanian, and Turkish flags. The following February a protest strike took place with similar demands. Some 1,300 zinc and lead miners occupied their mines, many going on a hunger strike. Miners in Slovenia and unionists in Croatia sent messages of support.

The Stalinist rulers in Belgrade responded with a deeply chauvinist campaign, claiming that Kosovo was part of a Serb "homeland" and that Albanians "breed too much." They circulated false stories of rape of Serbian women by Albanians in Kosovo.

They mobilized demonstrations of hundreds of thousands in Belgrade with a lynch-mob atmosphere against the people of

,sovo. After whipping up this wave of Serbian nationalism, the Belgrade government revoked what autonomy Kosovo previously had.

The bureaucracy in Croatia and Slovenia supported Belgrade's crackdown against Kosovo. All the bureaucrats had been shaken by the worker resistance of the previous years. In the first six months of 1988 there had been 800 strikes involving 150,000 people across Yugoslavia.

The rulers in Croatia and Slovenia orchestrated their own nationalist mobilizations, eventually holding plebiscites for independent statehood that received a majority of votes. The Belgrade government countered with further appeals to Serbian nationalism, arguing in favor of "Yugoslavia" and in the same breath for Serbian ascendancy.

*   *   *

These events reflect the crisis of bureaucratic rule in the context of the absence of any independent working-class leadership in Yugoslavia.

What is decisive for the working class is not merely its strength in relation to the bureaucratic rulers, but its understanding of its historic line of march as part of an international class, and of who are its allies in this struggle.

The Yugoslav revolution itself represented a giant stride in that direction for the workers and peasants. This is the direction working people there need to take up again, by organizing themselves to sweep away the parasitic bureaucracy that has led them to the disastrous position they are in today, and replacing it with a government of workers and farmers.

The revolution that is required in Yugoslavia is a *political* revolution, which differs from the revolution needed in capitalist

ARGIRIS MALAPANIS/MILITANT

Antiwar protesters in Belgrade, part of the hundreds of thousands who marched in Serbia in June and July 1992 protesting the regime's involvement in the war in Croatia and Bosnia.

countries only in the sense that working people will, in the course of overthrowing the bureaucratic caste and its system of domination, safeguard and build on the achievements of the first, anticapitalist revolution. Those conquests are nationalized property in the basic means of production, wholesale trade, and banking; the state monopoly of foreign trade; and the consequent capacity for economic planning.

In order to carry through the political revolution, a vanguard party must be forged by the most politically conscious, active, and self-sacrificing workers in the factories and fields, a party conscious of the line of march of the working class and drawing on the lessons of past struggles to point the way forward—a communist party. Such a vanguard party can draw in others committed to this working-class perspective.

The last thing the people of Yugoslavia need is an imperialist military intervention, which on whatever basis it begins will end up being turned against them. Sections of working people in Yugoslavia have already shown by their own actions the potential they possess to place their stamp on events:

• The hundreds of thousands who have protested against the war in Belgrade and elsewhere in Serbia;

• the refusal by as many as 50 percent of those called up for the draft under the rule of Belgrade to fight in the "Yugoslav" army against fellow working people in Slovenia and Croatia;

• the mothers of soldiers from Serbia who joined their Croatian counterparts in Zagreb in opposition to Belgrade's war against Slovenia;

• the fraternization between soldiers of the Yugoslav army and those they were sent to fight in Slovenia;

• the preparedness of large numbers of Sarajevo citizens of Serbian and Croatian origin to defend their city side by side with their Muslim brothers and sisters against the rightist cutthroat gangs of the Serbian nationalist forces.

All these are examples of the class solidarity that powered the Yugoslav revolution and that can point the way forward again.

Rather than imperialist intervention, what working people in Yugoslavia need above all is time to engage in politics—to test out leaderships, organizations, and programs that can advance their interests. Out of these experiences, and through contact with class-conscious fighters throughout the world, a new vanguard can be forged.

This vanguard will lead the struggle to overthrow the bureaucratic regime, reach out to workers around the world in the process, and take up the march toward socialism as part of this international struggle.

WILL MILITARY INTERVENTION STOP THE SLAUGHTER?

Will military intervention stop the slaughter?

by *Argiris Malapanis*

As the death toll of civilians in Bosnia-Herzegovina continues to mount, calls for outside military intervention, ostensibly to end the slaughter, are also growing. These include calls by organizations that claim to speak in the interests of working people.

The AFL-CIO sponsored a rally on August 26, 1992, in front of the Yugoslav embassy in Washington, D.C. Top union officials backed proposals by Democratic presidential contender Bill Clinton for U.S. intervention in Yugoslavia. "Do we have to wait for another Hitler to resurface before we do anything to help these people?" asked William Bywater, International Union of Electronic Workers (IUE) president, in a press release commenting on the rally.

In a center spread feature in the August 12, 1992, issue of the *Guardian,* a weekly newspaper published in New York, Jill Benderly and Evan Kraft argue that the "world" must intervene militarily in Bosnia to put an end to the slaughter.

Whatever their intentions—whether they give outright support to the bipartisan foreign-policy goals of the U.S. capitalist class, or are confused over how to stop the devastation working people face in former Yugoslavia—these forces end up calling on the same government that acts for a handful of wealthy families who rule the United States to intervene to "save" working people in the Balkans.

But history has proven that military intervention by Washington or other imperialist powers anywhere in the world wreaks havoc on workers and farmers. Arguments like those presented by the *Guardian* authors go in the opposite direction of the only way working people can advance: by organizing themselves as a class to act in defense of the interests of the toiling majority of humanity.

Following a reporting visit for the *Militant* to Belgrade, Zagreb, Split, Dubrovnik, and Sarajevo in July 1992, this reporter spoke at public forums on the Yugoslav war in Montreal, New York, and Philadelphia. Each time, questions were raised from the audience similar to those posed in the *Guardian* article.

Is it true that continued slaughter and imperialist military intervention are the only alternatives working people in the former Yugoslavia face? Is there a "world" or an "international community" that can act in the interests of the people of Bosnia? Is the United Nations an "international peacekeeping organization"? What is the cause of the strife in Yugoslavia? What can working people there do, if anything, to affect the course of events?

These questions are on the minds of working people in the United States and throughout the world, as they continue to watch on TV stark pictures of violence against fellow workers of all nationalities in Bosnia.

"The brutal and muddled war," write Kraft and Benderly, "has led many progressives, including ourselves, to feel for the first time ever a strong desire to see the world intercede militarily—to stop the murder in Bosnia." They express hope that "the United Nations, the European Community, and Washington will heed Bosnian pleas for military assistance."

First of all, there is no such thing as "the world" that can intervene in Bosnia; there are specific *governments* that defend particular class interests. In the capitalist countries of North America, Europe, and much of the rest of the world, the capitalist class owns the mines, mills, factories, banks, and most of the land, and it wields political power over the state to defend those class interests and property relations. The world is further divided into a handful of imperialist countries whose ruling classes dominate and super-exploit the overwhelming majority of the rest of humanity in the semicolonial world.

It is these imperialist powers—the *Guardian* names one, Washington—that are debating the merits of direct military intervention, organized and led by them, in Bosnia-Herzegovina, not some classless "world." The governments of the United States, Britain, France, Italy, Germany, and Japan have a long history of using their massive armed forces against the struggles of working people the world over.

The U.S. invasions of Panama (1989-90) and Grenada (1983), London's war against Argentina to maintain its colonization of the Malvinas Islands (1982), and the 1991 U.S-led war against the people of Iraq are simply the most recent examples.

Many see the United Nations as something distinct from the imperialist powers that control it. But contrary to Benderly and Kraft's implication, the UN has never been a mechanism, effective or otherwise, for the maintenance of international peace and security.

The UN was established on the terms of the victors in the most bloody and destructive interimperialist war the world has seen, World War II. The Allied capitalist regimes of the United States, Britain, and France had emerged supreme over the Axis governments of Germany, Japan, and Italy.

In that war, despite the reactionary course of the Stalinist regime in Moscow, also part of the Allied military coalition, the workers and farmers of the Soviet Union—at the cost of tens of millions of lives—succeeded in turning back the onslaught of German imperialism aimed at subjugating them once again to direct capitalist exploitation.

As the Allied powers neared victory in April 1945, the UN was set up to give a stamp of legitimacy to the postwar international status quo. U.S. president Franklin Roosevelt, British prime minister Winston Churchill, and Soviet premier Joseph Stalin met in Yalta in the Soviet Union to divide up the world into spheres of influence. Behind closed doors the national self-determination of peoples and countries and the interests of workers and farmers the world over were trampled into the dust.

These three governments were the true "United Nations" at its birth. Their mutual veto privileges in the Security Council established a framework in which they could continue to advance their common interests, while blocking each other where their interests diverged. Subsequently the initial Big Three were expanded to a Big Five, including the governments of France and China.

At the opening of the 1950s Washington organized the massive invasion of Korea under the blue flag of the UN. Imperialist troops fought the entire 1950–53 Korean War with a Security Council mandate, with the result that the forcible division of the Korean peninsula against the will of the big majority of its people was extended and reinforced. U.S. troops, stationed along the border that divides Korea today, still fly the UN flag.

In 1961 UN forces were complicit in the assassination of Patrice Lumumba, prime minister of the African country of the Congo (now Zaire), who had led that country's independence struggle from Belgium. Faced with a secessionist movement organized by the former Belgian rulers, Lumumba himself appealed to the UN to send a peacekeeping force to help defend the newly established independent government.

Washington voted for Lumumba's request for UN troops in the Security Council, as did the four other permanent members. At the very same time, according to a 1975 U.S. Senate report, the CIA was plotting Lumumba's assassination as "an urgent and prime objective," in the words of then CIA director Allen Dulles. The Senate report accepted as a "reasonable inference" that the order to kill the Congolese leader came directly from President Dwight Eisenhower.

Many of the UN-sponsored troops were supplied by the government of Sweden, an imperialist regime that was often touted as "neutralist" and "pro–Third World." When they arrived in the Congo, the UN troops refused to take any action against the local rightist forces. Instead they disarmed Lumumba's troops and stood by while his government was ousted by the Belgian- and U.S.-sponsored forces, and while Lumumba himself—who had come to symbolize the anticolonial fight to millions in Africa and around the world—was murdered in cold blood.

Washington's war against the people of Iraq was the largest military operation to take place with UN Security Council endorsement since the Korean War.

Recalling the U.S.-led war against Iraq, the *Guardian* authors acknowledge that the prospect of a similar intervention in Yugoslavia "stirs fears of another nasty bombing mission and botched political aftermath sponsored by the global rent-a-cop."

But they continue: "To us, international intervention, with all the geopolitical implications it brings, is preferable to standing by indifferently as villages are destroyed, civilians killed by land mines and shoppers gunned down trying to buy the few groceries available to them."

What are the "geopolitical implications"? Leaving aside the muddleheadedness expressed in such terms, what in fact were the implications—or, better, the consequences—of the U.S.-led war against Iraq?

As many as 150,000 human beings were slaughtered. In February 1991, as Iraqi soldiers and civilians were fleeing from Kuwait City to Basra, the U.S.-led forces closed the highway at both ends and simply kept bombing and shelling every person, jeep, truck, car, and bicycle. The carnage on the road to Basra ranks among the worst atrocities of modern warfare.

When, later on, hundreds of thousands of Kurdish people were forced to flee Saddam Hussein's terror in northern Iraq, neither Washington nor other imperialist governments opened their borders to Kurdish refugees. Thousands of Iraqi working people, including many children, lost their lives because of the two-year-long embargo imposed on Iraq with UN camouflage. This is what George Bush and Bill Clinton are preparing to repeat in Iraq with the imposition of the "no-fly zone" south of the thirty-second parallel.

The "European Community" that the *Guardian* authors also place hopes in took an active part in the Iraqi massacre.

The rival imperialist powers of North America and Europe are seeking ways to intervene in the Yugoslav war and place their stamp on the outcome of events. They are driven to do this by increased conflicts among themselves in the context of a world capitalist economy marked by declining profit rates and stiffening competition for markets for commodities and capital.

The ruling families of the United States, Germany, Britain, and France are contemplating military intervention in Bosnia not to stop atrocities in prison camps or the continued bombardment of Sarajevo, Gorazde, and other Bosnian cities. Their hearts go out only to cold cash, not human misery.

Washington is considering intervention to block its imperialist rivals in Europe from getting a firmer economic foothold in the former Yugoslavia. In fact, the U.S. government initially sought to avert the breakup of Yugoslavia to avoid instability that it feared would work to the advantage of its rivals. Washington worries that the U.S.-dominated NATO might lose its ability to call all the shots over military matters in Europe to one or another institution dominated by Bonn and Paris.

Particular imperialist governments have forged links to the Croatian regime of President Franjo Tudjman, others to Serbian president Slobodan Milosevic. German capital, for example, has developed a bigger stake in Croatia than in other former republics of Yugoslavia. Only after Bonn got its foot in the door by open support to the Croatian regime did Washington recognize Bosnia-Herzegovina as an independent state and begin talking about intervention.

The hypocrisy of the imperialist governments' professed humanitarian concerns is most glaring in their stance towards the millions of refugees fleeing the carnage. London has expelled refugees seeking asylum, while Paris and Washington have allowed in only a few hundred.

"The kind of intervention that seems most sensible would be to arm the Bosnians against the Serbs," says the *Guardian* article. "At the moment the across-the-board arms embargo on the region—though porous—gives the already well-stocked Yugoslav army a tremendous advantage."

The people of Sarajevo and other Bosnian towns who are defending themselves against "ethnic cleansing" have the right to get weapons wherever they can. The labor movement in the United States and elsewhere should oppose the arms embargo as well as the inhuman economic sanctions imposed on the people of Serbia and Montenegro.

But that is a different story from calling on the U.S. ruling class to "arm the Bosnians." The *Guardian* authors turn their eyes, once again, toward the very same class that is responsible for the oppression and exploitation of working people not only in Yugoslavia but around the world.

More than forty-five years ago Yugoslav workers and peasants led a successful revolution to win land, democratic rights, and better social conditions. In the process they forged working-class unity that cut across ethnic and religious lines. They did so in a mighty struggle—led by an armed movement called the Partisans—against the local landlords and capitalists, as well as the imperialist powers of Europe and the United States.

In their successful struggle to overthrow capitalism and establish a workers' and farmers' government, Yugoslav toilers fought against imperialist powers like Germany, Britain, and France, which had dominated the country, much like a colony, prior to World War II. Following the war, with the aid of Moscow, Washington and London successfully blocked the victory of a workers' and farmers' regime in neighboring Greece but were not strong enough to force back the revolution in Yugoslavia.

Yet these are the same capitalist powers that the *Guardian* authors are calling upon to rescue working people in Bosnia today.

In a statement opposing U.S. military intervention in Yugoslavia, the Communist Party USA (CPUSA) argues that "Yugoslavia's dismantling" was caused by "the internal meddling of German and U.S. imperialism." Similar statements appear in the pages of *Workers World,* weekly newspaper of the Workers World Party.

Their position is simply a coverup for the crimes of the Stalinist murder machine in Yugoslavia, whose rival wings are now tearing the country apart. Into this situation, the competing imperialist powers of Europe and North America are of course seeking ways to intervene. But imperialist intervention was not the *cause* of the breakup of Yugoslavia.

The CPUSA and its newspaper, the *People's Weekly World,* echo the rationalizations for the current carnage put forward by the Milosevic regime in Serbia, which the CPUSA supports. An article by Tom Foley in the July 18, 1992, issue, for example, argues that Muslims in Bosnia are for the most part privileged heirs of the landlord class that ruled the region during the Ottoman Empire.

This is absurd. As if "Muslims" in Bosnia are responsible for the crimes of the Ottoman Empire. Are "Serbs," then, accountable for the crimes of the pre-World War II Karageorgevich monarchy? Should "Croats" be held collectively guilty for the crimes of the fascist Ustashi movement in World War II?

In the same article Foley supports the division of Bosnia into cantons—that is, into "autonomous" regions supposedly divided along national lines—as a way to stop the war. This proposal has been put forward by the regimes in Serbia and Croatia as a thinly veiled cover for a land grab. It has also been backed by ruling-class spokespeople in the United States and various European countries.

The last thing the people of Yugoslavia need is imperialist military intervention or economic sanctions.

From the beginning of the bloody war in 1991, layers of the working class in Yugoslavia have shown by their own actions the potential they possess to resist the slaughter and the horrors of "ethnic cleansing."

Hundreds of thousands of students and workers have protested against the war in Belgrade. Thousands of young people have refused to fight in the "Yugoslav" army against fellow working people in Slovenia, Croatia, and Bosnia.

Mothers of soldiers from Serbia organized joint demonstrations with their Croatian counterparts in Zagreb demanding their sons be brought back from Slovenia.

Some of the biggest antiwar demonstrations took place in Sarajevo in March 1992, before the siege of the city began. Since then, large numbers of Sarajevo citizens of Serbian and Croatian origin have fought alongside their Muslim brothers and sisters against the rightist gangs of the Serbian Democratic Party that are

Students in Belgrade protest against the war, July 1992.

indiscriminately shelling the city.

Will working people in Yugoslavia be able to replace the rival gangs in power with their own government and put an end to the war? That depends above all on progress toward forging a working-class leadership with a clear political perspective. Reliance on their own independent organization—not on any wing of the caste, nor any capitalist government—is the only road forward. Working people in Yugoslavia need time and the freedom to put different leaderships and perspectives to the test.

In their fight to end the onslaught, they do need and deserve international solidarity. Calls for imperialist military intervention issued by forces linked to the labor movement in the United States are a blow not only against workers in the Balkans but weaken the working class and the labor movement in this country as well.

Instead, working people and the unions in the United States and the world over should demand:

End all plans for military intervention in Bosnia!

Lift economic sanctions against Serbia and Montenegro, as well as the arms embargo against all the former Yugoslav republics!

Send massive food and medical aid to the besieged people of Sarajevo and other Bosnian towns!

Open the U.S. and other imperialist borders to the refugees from the Yugoslav carnage!

REPORT FROM KOSOVO

Report from Kosovo

by Anne Howie and Natasha Terlexis

From the moment you enter Kosovo, tension is palpably in the air. At the approach to the area's main city, Pristina, all incoming and outgoing vehicles are stopped, boarded by armed police, and checked for young men evading the draft.

Kosovo is a plateau of good farmland surrounded by mountains. Ninety percent of its two million inhabitants are ethnic Albanians. As Yugoslavia disintegrates, a tug-of-war is going on over demands for independence raised by many Albanians in hopes of a better future and the attempts by the government of Serbia to maintain its control over the region.

The village homes in the area are built in the traditional manner, with interior courtyards surrounded by high walls. This predominantly agricultural area has seen considerable industrial development in the past four decades. It was a major producer of electricity for the former Yugoslavia and is the site of coal and other mines.

Today factories surrounding Pristina seem to be closed for the most part, with broken windows and tall grass in the yards. Around a stark center of government buildings wind communities of prefabricated housing dotted with small shops and cafes. Police guards in town carry automatic weapons and a tank stands at the entrance of the police station. Photographs of the city center are not permitted.

The victorious Partisan struggle against Nazi occupation in World War II turned into a deep-going revolution, actively involving hundreds of thousands in Yugoslavia. Farmers and working people of all nationalities, including Albanians, participated. By the mid-1940s the vast bulk of the country's industry had been nationalized, while 95 percent of arable land was distributed to small peasants who previously had none.

In the years that followed, Albanians were recognized as a distinct national group for the first time, their language became one of Yugoslavia's official languages, and Albanians won the right to education in their own language.

The country's first five-year plan was inaugurated in 1947, including an allocation of additional resources to the more economically backward regions of Yugoslavia.

Flaka Surroi, member of the Council for the Defense of Human Rights and Freedoms, based in Pristina, says that Kosovo realized its highest level of economic development following these measures.

In spite of this, Kosovo remains the poorest region of the former Yugoslavia. According to Mihailo Markovich, vice president of the ruling Serbian Socialist Party, if the average of leading economic indicators for all republics in 1980 were 100, then Kosovo would be at 28 as compared with Slovenia at 230. In the early 1980s the economic situation began to deteriorate, Surroi explains.

In 1974 Kosovo was granted autonomous status following demonstrations demanding a republic.

"In 1981 student demonstrations revived the demand for the status of a republic within the federal state of Yugoslavia," Surroi said. "Such ideas were met with increasing repression." The authorities claimed the Albanian government was behind these demands. Writing the slogan "Kosovo Republic" carried a sentence of six years, according to the Minority Rights Group based in London.

Since 1981 Serbs and Montenegrins have emigrated from Kosovo, accusing ethnic Albanians of intimidation. Since 1985 the situation of Serbs in Kosovo began to feature prominently in the Serbian press, the rights group says. In 1987, 60,000 Serbs signed a petition alleging "genocide" against Serbs in Kosovo.

The Minority Rights Group reports that "there appears to be no basis for the highly emotive charge of genocide."

In the 1990 elections in Serbia, the former Communist Party, renamed the Serbian Socialist Party, won by a landslide. President Slobodan Milosevic ran on a program of uniting Serbia once again, protecting Serb minorities in other republics, and deepening moves toward the market system. The same year regimes led by demagogues using similar nationalist rhetoric came to power in other regions of the former Yugoslavia.

In Serbia, the alliance of opposition parties that is presenting a program of ousting the Milosevic government and stepping up efforts to stop the war in Bosnia shares the view that Kosovo should remain part of the republic of Serbia.

In 1988 the Serbian government began the process of changing the constitution of Serbia, in order to eliminate Kosovo's autonomous status. In July of 1990, Belgrade cracked down further, dissolving the Kosovo parliament.

Strikes and demonstrations rocked the area in response to each turning point in the process, followed by more repressive measures against the population.

"Five hundred thousand Albanians demonstrated in Pristina in November 1989," says Surroi. This was followed by strikes of construction, mine, and other workers.

The Independent Trade Union of Kosovo (ITU) was formed

in 1989. Starting with construction workers, it began to recruit members in all industries and services, disillusioned by the unions dominated by the former Communist Party, which were not seen as representing the interests of workers of Albanian origin.

The membership of ITU, according to Surroi, includes "only a small number of Serbs, maybe four or five." The ITU, in September 1990, organized a one-day strike protesting the new labor law. "Most of industry shut down, and 3,000 private shops as well. But in the following months, 64,000 workers were dismissed, and many shops were forced to close for six months to a year." Surroi explains that it is no small matter for the union to function today, since it has "200,000 members—all of them fired."

Workers dismissed have "no access to any form of social security payments." Many live on food sent to the towns by relatives and others in the countryside. Thousands have sought work abroad.

Surroi stated that 1,657 medical personnel have been dismissed, all Albanians, leading to the closure of thirty-eight clinics in Pristina alone. "Many medics now work on a voluntary basis."

For more than a year now, schools teaching in the Albanian language—from elementary schools to Pristina's university—have been closed. Previously, Kosovo had a parallel school system in both Albanian and Serbo-Croatian through all levels of education.

"The Albanians are not going to school because they don't want to study the history of Serbia," a Pristina-area high school student of Serbian origin said in an interview. "But they live in this country, they have to."

Surroi, on the other hand, said that the Serbian government introduced a new curriculum that was not accepted by Albanian teachers. "They were asked to sign a loyalty oath to Serbia, and were fired on refusal." Despite the fact that their diplomas are not recognized, says Surroi, students continue to receive instruction and to graduate out of the private homes of volunteer teachers.

A report issued by the Council for the Defense of Human Rights and Freedoms states that "since 1989 the Serbian police and army arbitrarily killed ninety-six Albanians, mostly young people. Eighteen of the victims were minors. No police officers or soldiers have been arrested."

Many Albanian youth are due to be drafted into the army of Yugoslavia, which now comprises just Serbia and Montenegro. "Nobody wants to join up," says Surroi.

The UN sanctions against Serbia are hitting the people of Kosovo hard, after the economic dislocations of the past several years. "People are really suffering now. The economic base just keeps going down and down," she says.

THE QUESTION OF MACEDONIA
A DISCUSSION FROM THE PAGES OF THE 'MILITANT'

Why Greek rulers refuse to recognize rights of Macedonia

by Argiris Malapanis

Readers B.M. and G.K. comment in the letters section this week on *Militant* articles about demands for independence by the Yugoslav republic of Macedonia and the Greek government's opposition to it.

The government of the republic of Macedonia raised the demand for independence following the de facto breakup of Yugoslavia through the ongoing conflict there.

The conflict is a result of decades of bureaucratic rule by the Stalinist regime in Yugoslavia. A deep-going and popular revolution coming out of World War II began to break down the divisions between the peoples of Yugoslavia—whether Serbs, Croats, Slovenes, Albanians, Montenegrins, Macedonians, or others. These divisions were fostered by imperialism and the native capitalists.

Steps through struggle to further the unity of working people were blocked by the Stalinist regime. As a result of the growing social and economic crisis over the past decade, ruling layers in the various regions have been pressing to enhance their own position and access to resources through force and violence.

While great numbers of people in different parts of Yugoslavia have been drawn into the fighting, voices continue to be heard against the war. Thousands of Belgrade students, for example, demonstrated in early March 1992 demanding Serbian president Slobodan Milosevic's resignation for his role in spurring the civil war.

The bureaucratic rulers of the republic of Macedonia have the same narrow goals as their Serb or Croatian counterparts. The attitude of communists toward demands for independence depends on whether a fight for such demands advances the interests of working people in a particular country. What is needed to advance working-class interests is a fight aimed at uniting workers in different parts of Yugoslavia, Greece, Bulgaria, and throughout the region.

A necessary part of such a fight for unity is the struggle against the oppression of any nationality, including the suppression of languages, culture, or religions.

Before World War II, under the rule of King Alexander I, a Serb, Macedonians were forbidden by law to publish books or newspapers in their native language. This was reversed by the Yugoslav revolution, which championed the demands of oppressed nationalities. Following the overturn of capitalist rule in Yugoslavia, the Macedonian language was recognized and in fact it is now written and standardized, contrary to what G.K. asserts. It is a dialect of the Slavic language spoken in Bulgaria. Working people in the republic of Macedonia fought to preserve their language and to be allowed to use it.

Progressive measures were taken during the initial stages of the Yugoslav revolution to develop the economy of underdeveloped Macedonia. As a result, while industrial output in the more advanced regions of Croatia, Slovenia, and Serbia increased nine or tenfold from 1939 to 1970, in Macedonia the increase was more than thirtyfold.

It was the example of this revolution that the Greek bourgeoisie and other capitalist classes in the region feared. B.M. correctly points out that a blow was dealt to Greek imperialism's plans to conquer Macedonia at the end of World War II.

Hatred for the Yugoslav revolution and what it accomplished comes through even today in arguments raised by spokespeople of the Greek ruling class to justify their opposition to recognition of Macedonia.

For example, in an open letter to the European Community, former Greek minister of culture Melina Mercouri and five other well-known personalities in Greece stated:

> You of course are aware of the effort begun earlier and system-atized after 1944 with the creation, in the framework of the Federal People's Republic of Yugoslavia, of the so-called state of "Macedonia." Its single goal, then and now, was the ques-tioning of the borders of Greece, within which is included Greek Macedonia . . . with a homogeneous Greek population.

Recent demonstrations in Salonika and in New York, spon-sored by the Greek government, raised the slogan "Macedonia was, is, and will remain Greek." This is similar to such slogans as "America for the Americans" or "France first" advanced by incip-ient fascist currents in the United States, France, and other imperi-alist countries.

As G.K. points out, there are oppressed nationalities in north-ern Greece, and indeed throughout the country, including hundreds of thousands of undocumented immigrant workers, many of them from the Balkans. One of these is the Macedonian nationality, com-prising about 2 percent of the population of Greece. As B. M. notes, many are treated by the state as "agents of Skopje" (the capital of Macedonia) for attempting to use their language or their culture.

Communists and other fighters in Greece have in the past been charged with "treason" because they championed demands against the national oppression of Macedonians. One of them was Pantelis Pouliopoulos, national secretary of the Communist Party (KKE), until he was expelled in 1927 for his opposition to the counterrevolutionary course of Stalin. He was jailed twice by the Greek government for his proletarian stance on the Macedonian question—in 1924 and in 1928.

*   *   *

Since the column above appeared in the *Militant* in April 1992, the conservative government of Constantínos Mitsotákis has stepped up its international campaign against recognition of the former Yugoslav republic of Macedonia. The social democratic opposition and most trade union officials in Greece have given their full backing to the effort.

On December 9, 1992, more than one million people participated in a rally in Athens to back the government's campaign. "Macedonia has been Greek for 3,000 years," shouted many in the crowd. The absurdity of this slogan becomes apparent when one considers that during this time span millions of people of different nationalities, speaking a spectrum of languages, and living under various social systems, have inhabited the area comprising what is today the republic of Macedonia and northern Greece.

Athens, however, has used such slogans to whip up nationalist sentiments and win backing among working people for its goals. In the course of this campaign the Greek government has carried out sweeping attacks on democratic rights.

On May 6, 1992, four activists of the Antiwar–Antinationalist Campaign of Greece were fined and sentenced to nineteen months in jail each after being arrested for passing out leaflets opposing the government's position on Macedonia. "The neighboring people of Macedonia are not our enemy. No to nationalism and war," was the main slogan on the flier.

A few months earlier six people were sentenced to six months in jail each for putting up posters with the slogan "Recognize independent Slav Macedonia." Several students have been expelled from high schools for advocating similar positions.

In another case, the government has charged five members of a group, the Organization for Socialist Revolution, with "exposing the friendly relations of Greece with foreign countries to the risk of disturbance" and "inciting citizens to rivalry and division." The evidence? A pamphlet titled *The Crisis in the Balkans, the Macedonian Question, and the Working Class.* The booklet opposes the government's position on Macedonia.

"If the government can get away with this, it would be deadly for the labor movement," Vageliό Sotiropoulou, one of the four members of the Antiwar Campaign who were arrested and convicted, said in an interview in Athens in July 1992. The four are out on bail while appealing the court's decision. Supporters of democratic rights the world over should join in demanding that these convictions be overturned and the charges dropped.

The Greek government has continued its nationalist campaign on Macedonia. But recently, under pressure from Washington, Bonn, and Paris, it was forced to accept a compromise. On April 8, 1993, the United Nations Security Council approved UN membership for Macedonia under the name "Former Yugoslav Republic of Macedonia."

Argiris Malapanis
May 1993

Is there a Macedonian nationality?

Letter from G.K.

The *Militant* in the March 13, 1992, issue correctly criticizes the European Community (EC) for bowing to Greek capitalist demands that the Yugoslav republic of Macedonia be denied independent recognition. It also spotlights ambitions the Athens government has harbored in the past for areas of southern Yugoslavia and Bulgaria.

But one must correct the *Militant* on the question of a separate Macedonian nationality, which the article implies. There is no such thing! No Macedonian language, no Macedonian ethnic group, no Macedonian literature. In fact the majority of the people in Yugoslav Macedonia are of Bulgarian origin and speak Slavic, since the Bulgarian language disappeared centuries ago. The inhabitants of Greek Macedonia speak Greek. Greek Macedonia, the origin of Alexander the Great and the Hellenistic dynasties of the Ancient Middle East, whose rule the generals of Alexander's army spawned, the rule of the Ptolemies and Cleopatra in Egypt being the most well-known, spoke a language—Greek in origin—similar to that spoken by the ancient Spartans.

In modern times, after the forced deportation of almost two million Greeks from Asia Minor and the Pontus (the area around the Black Sea), Salonika and Greek Macedonia, where most of the refugees settled, became a center of radical resistance to the capitalist designs of the Athens government, and where many refugees, traumatized by the "Asia Minor Catastrophe," turned to the Greek Communist Party and Socialist left for leadership.

There are of course ethnic minorities in Greek Macedonia, as well as in Thrace and Thessaly, whose rights the nationalist capitalist regimes in Athens, whether royalist or republican, have never protected. But that is a different question from implying the existence of a separate Macedonian nation. As far as I know, neither the inhabitants of Yugoslav or Greek Macedonia consider themselves a separate people.

In any case we can agree on the most important point. Greece should join Bulgaria and Turkey and *urge* rather than *obstruct* the EC's recognition of Yugoslav Macedonia. Athens should also pressure the nationalist bureaucracy ruling in Belgrade to let Yugoslav Macedonia determine its own destiny.

G.K.

New York, New York

No to chauvinist campaign against Macedonia
Letter from B.M.

A World News Briefs article in the *Militant* noted that the Greek government protested the declaration of independence by the Yugoslav republic of Macedonia, fearing that this "might give rise to demands for rights among the ethnic Macedonian minority in Greece."

The fact is that this oppressed minority has been raising their national demands in Greece for decades. Much like the Kurds, the Macedonians were divided by imperialism and the local capitalists within the borders of what became Bulgaria, Greece, and Yugoslavia. In World War II, Greek imperialism aimed to conquer Macedonia but a deadly blow to this plan was the armed struggle of the Macedonians, which culminated in the formation of their republic as part of the Yugoslav federation in 1945.

With the crushing of the Greek revolution in 1949 and the

subsequent sealing of the border, almost every Macedonian family in the province of Florina to this day has relatives on the other side who are not allowed to come to Greece. They are subjected to terror by the police in Greece, who see anyone who speaks Macedonian, who sings their traditional songs, or dances their traditional dances as "an agent of Skopje."

The Greek government has been whipping up nationalist chauvinism to convince working people to look for the wrong enemy. This reactionary campaign, supported by all major political parties, the union bureaucracy, women's and youth organizations, and the church, resulted in a march of one million in Salonika at the beginning of March 1992 around the slogan "Macedonia is Greek."

Class-conscious workers face the task of explaining the imperialist aims of Greek capitalism and, while supporting the just demands of the Macedonians, they must demand: Open the borders to the republic of Macedonia now!

B. M.
Salonika, Greece

Index

FOR FURTHER READING_____

To See the Dawn

BAKU, 1920—FIRST CONGRESS OF THE PEOPLES OF THE EAST

Two thousand delegates from across Asia, convened by the Communist International, appealed to oppressed peoples to unite with revolutionary workers everywhere "for the liberation of all mankind from the yoke of capitalist and imperialist slavery!" The latest volume in the series *The Communist International in Lenin's Time.* $19.95

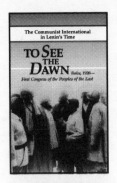

The History of the Russian Revolution

by Leon Trotsky

The social, economic, and political dynamics of the first victorious socialist revolution, as told by one of its central leaders. Unique in modern literature. Unabridged edition, 1369 pp. $35.95

The Communist Manifesto

by Karl Marx and Frederick Engels

Founding document, written in 1847, of the modern working-class movement. It explains how capitalism arose as a specific stage in the economic development of class society and how it will be superseded through the revolutionary action, on a world scale, of the working class. $2.50

The Revolution Betrayed

WHAT IS THE SOVIET UNION AND WHERE IS IT GOING?

by Leon Trotsky

Classic study of the degeneration of the Soviet workers' state under the domination of the privileged social caste whose spokesman was Stalin. Illuminates the roots of the crisis of the 1990s. $19.95

The Balkan Wars (1912-13)

THE WAR CORRESPONDENCE OF LEON TROTSKY

On-the-spot analysis of national and social conflicts in the Balkans, written 80 years ago, sheds light on the conflicts shaking these countries today. $32.95

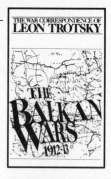

Communism and the Fight for a Popular Revolutionary Government: 1848 to Today

by Mary-Alice Waters

Traces the continuity in the fight by the working-class movement over the past 150 years to wrest political power from the small minority of wealthy property owners whose class rule is inseparably linked to misery and hunger for the great majority of humanity.
In *New International* no. 3. $8.00

Workers' and Farmers' Governments Since the Second World War

by Bob Chester

A study of the anticapitalist governments that came to power in the revolutions in Yugoslavia, China, Cuba, and Algeria. $6.00

The Workers' and Farmers' Government

by Joseph Hansen

A discussion of the social transformations carried out following revolutions in Eastern Europe, China, and Cuba, and the class character of the new governments established there. $7.00

Class, Party, and State and the Eastern European Revolution

Articles, resolutions, and debates discussing the social and political evolution of the governments that came to power in post-World War II revolutions in Eastern Europe. $7.00

WRITE FOR A FREE CATALOG

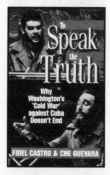
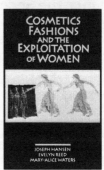

New International

A MAGAZINE OF MARXIST POLITICS AND THEORY

IN ISSUE 7

Opening Guns of World War III:

WASHINGTON'S ASSAULT ON IRAQ

BY JACK BARNES

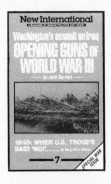

> The U.S. government's murderous blockade, bombardment, and invasion of Iraq heralded a period of increasingly sharp conflicts among imperialist powers, more wars, and growing instability of international capitalism. 333 pp., $12.00

IN ISSUE 8

Che Guevara, Cuba, and the Road to Socialism

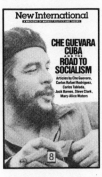

> Exchanges from both the early 1960s and today on the lasting importance and historical weight of the political and economic perspectives defended by Ernesto Che Guevara. 204 pp., $10.00

IN ISSUE 5

The Coming Revolution in South Africa

BY JACK BARNES

> The world importance of the struggle to overthrow the apartheid system and the vanguard role of the African National Congress, which is committed to lead the national, democratic revolution in South Africa to a successful conclusion.
> 198 pp., $9.00

IN ISSUE 6

The Second Assassination of Maurice Bishop

BY STEVE CLARK

> The accomplishments and lessons of the Grenada revolution, 1979-83, and how it was overthrown from within by the Stalinist gang that murdered Maurice Bishop. 272 pp., $10.00

DISTRIBUTED BY PATHFINDER